Aztecs, Incas & Mayans

Similarities and Differences

Ancient Civilization Book |
Fourth Grade Social Studies |
Children's Geography & Cultures Books

BABY PROFESSOR
EDUCATION KIDS

First Edition, 2019

Published in the United States by Speedy Publishing LLC, 40 E Main Street, Newark, Delaware 19711 USA.

© 2019 Baby Professor Books, an imprint of Speedy Publishing LLC

Baby Professor Books are available at special discounts when purchased in bulk for industrial and sales-promotional use. For details contact our Special Sales Team at Speedy Publishing LLC, 40 E Main Street, Newark, Delaware 19711 USA. Telephone (888) 248-4521 Fax: (210) 519-4043. www.speedybookstore.com

10 9 8 7 6 * 5 4 3 2 1

Print Edition: 9781541949850
Digital Edition: 9781541951655

See the world in pictures. Build your knowledge in style.
https://www.speedypublishing.com/

Contents

Aztec pyramid

Ancient Mayan city

Ancient Inca City

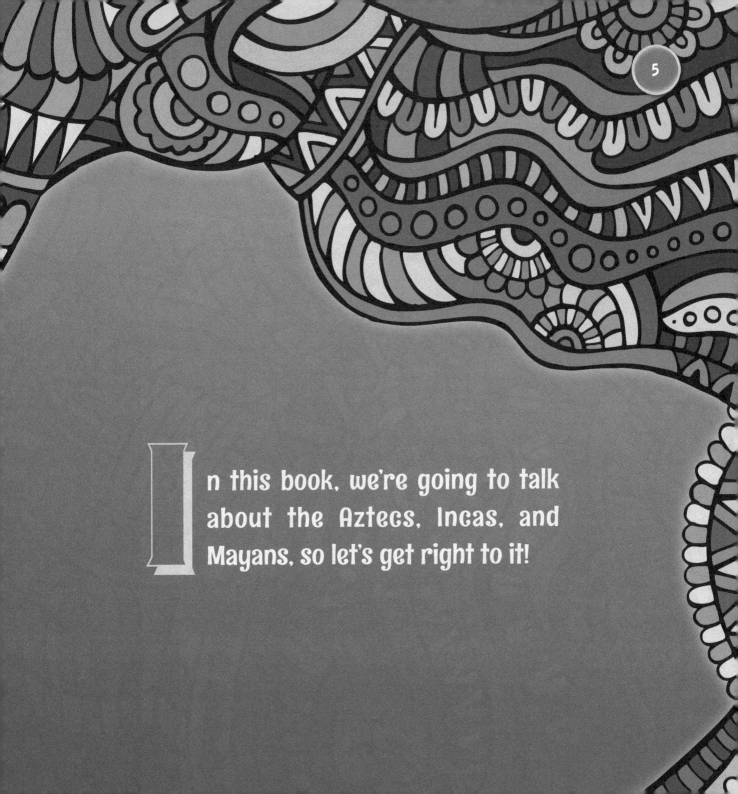

In this book, we're going to talk about the Aztecs, Incas, and Mayans, so let's get right to it!

How Did Geography Influence the Development of the Mayan, Incan, and Aztec Civilizations?

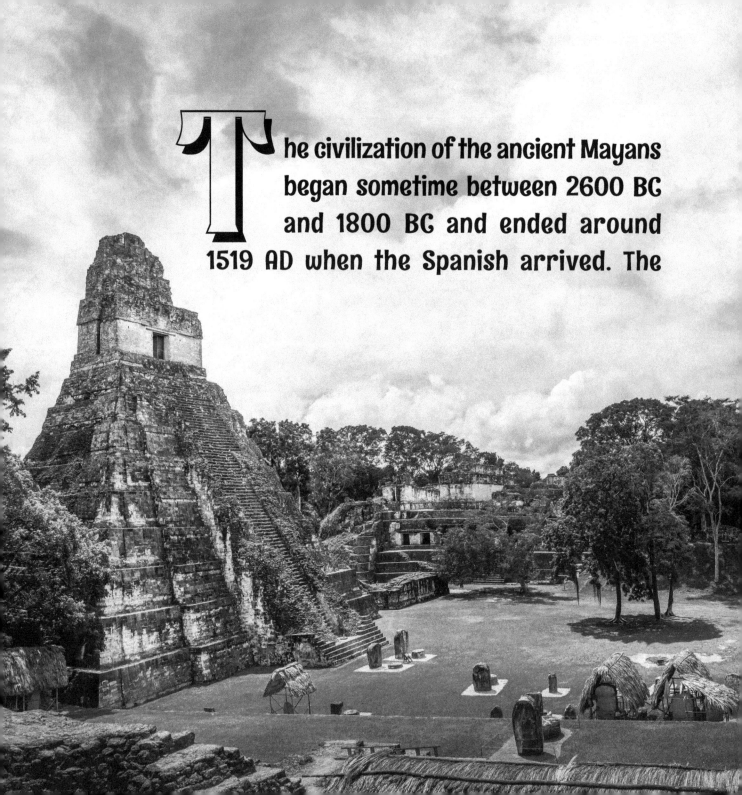

The civilization of the ancient Mayans began sometime between 2600 BC and 1800 BC and ended around 1519 AD when the Spanish arrived. The

Mayans spread out from the southern region of what is now Mexico to the northern section of Central America, which today is known as Guatemala, Belize, and Honduras.

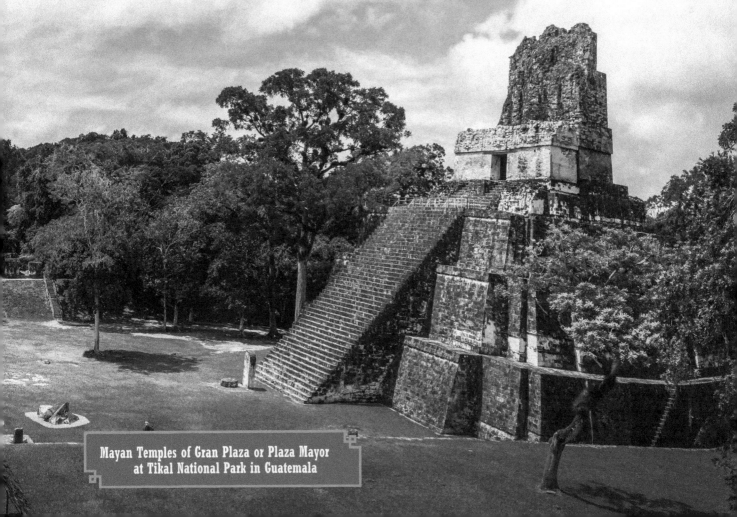

Mayan Temples of Gran Plaza or Plaza Mayor at Tikal National Park in Guatemala

Ancient Mayan pyramid of the lost city Calakmul surrounded by the green jungle of Campeche, Mexico

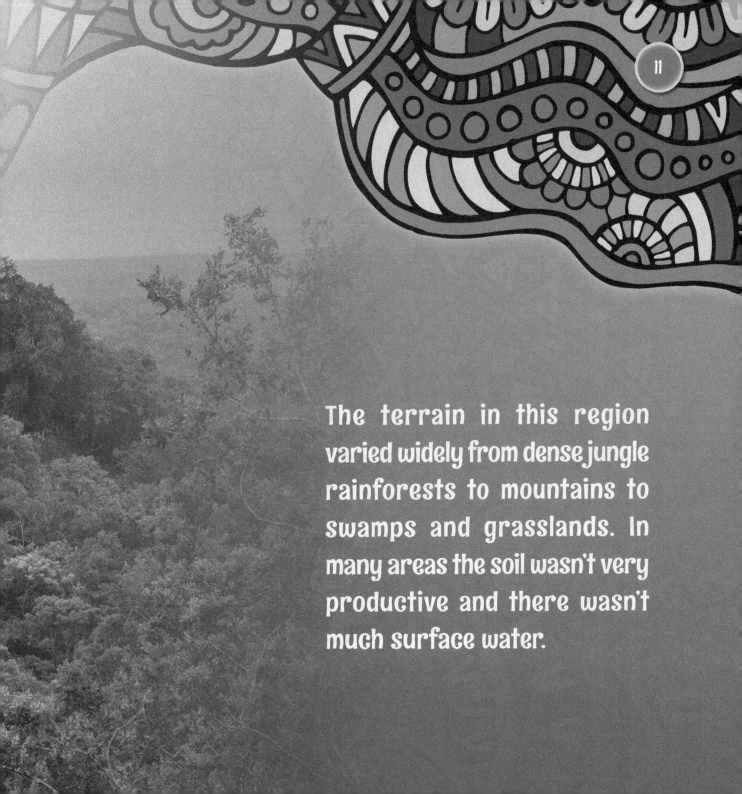

The terrain in this region varied widely from dense jungle rainforests to mountains to swamps and grasslands. In many areas the soil wasn't very productive and there wasn't much surface water.

These two factors made farming very difficult. However, that didn't stop the Mayans from cultivating maize and other crops. They came up with creative farming methods.

The civilization of the ancient Aztecs began around 1100 AD and ended around 1519 AD when the Spaniards arrived. They lived in what is now called the Valley of Mexico, which has an elevation of 8,000 feet above sea level.

The Valley of Mexico

Ancient Mexico City
and Lake Texcoco

They moved many times and around 900 AD they settled in one of the swampy islands in Lake Texcoco.

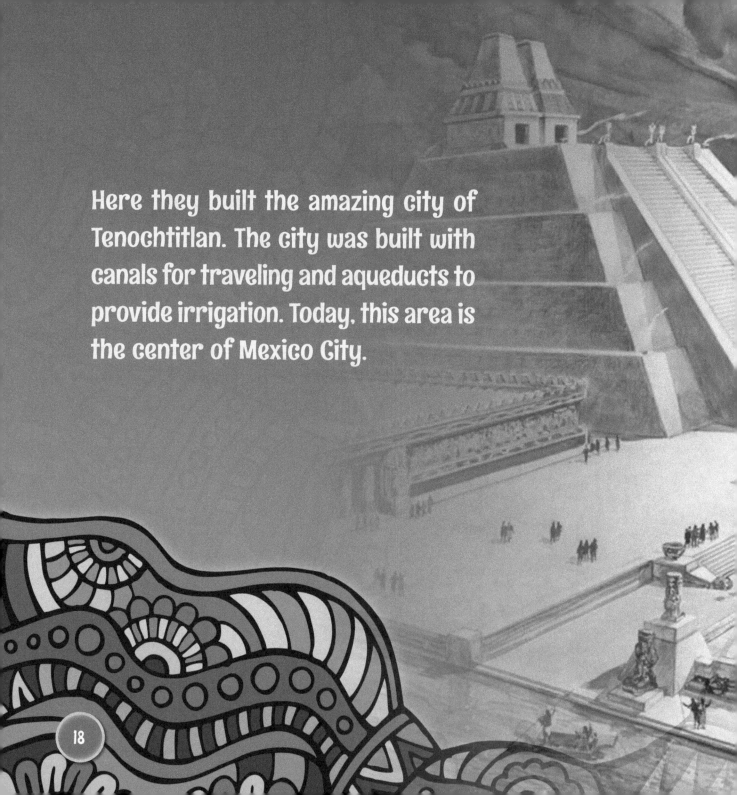

Here they built the amazing city of Tenochtitlan. The city was built with canals for traveling and aqueducts to provide irrigation. Today, this area is the center of Mexico City.

The lost Inca city, Machu Picchu in Cuzco, Peru

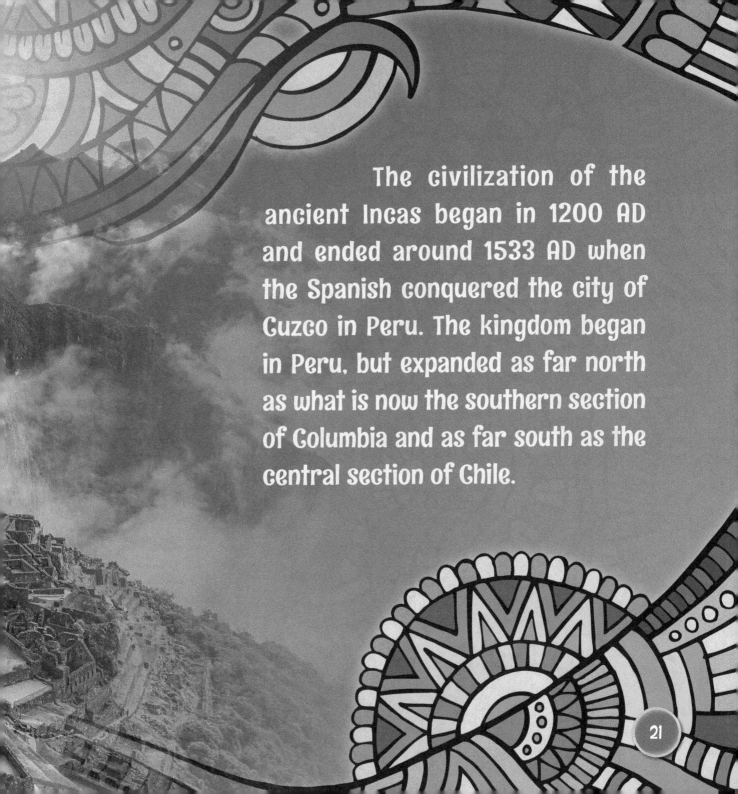

The civilization of the ancient Incas began in 1200 AD and ended around 1533 AD when the Spanish conquered the city of Cuzco in Peru. The kingdom began in Peru, but expanded as far north as what is now the southern section of Columbia and as far south as the central section of Chile.

Their empire was vast and stretched over the Andes Mountains. Cuzco was constructed in a valley that had been formed by glaciers. Three rivers intersected there, which made it perfect for farming. Their environment was filled with mountains, plains, deserts, jungles, and interlaced with rivers. They were creative farmers and they grew potatoes and corn.

The Inca empire was vast and stretched over the Andes Mountains

Similarities and Differences in Farming

All three civilizations were able to master their difficult terrains both for travel and for growing crops. Corn was a vital crop to all three and all three had ocean access as well as mountainous, high-elevation terrain. The terrain where the Incas were living in the Andes was the highest elevation. One of the main differences regarding farming was that the quality of soil was poor for the Mayans and fertile for the Aztecs.

Corn was a vital crop to the Incas, Mayans, and Aztecs

What Were the Achievements of the Maya, Aztec, and Inca?

Ancient Mayan calendar

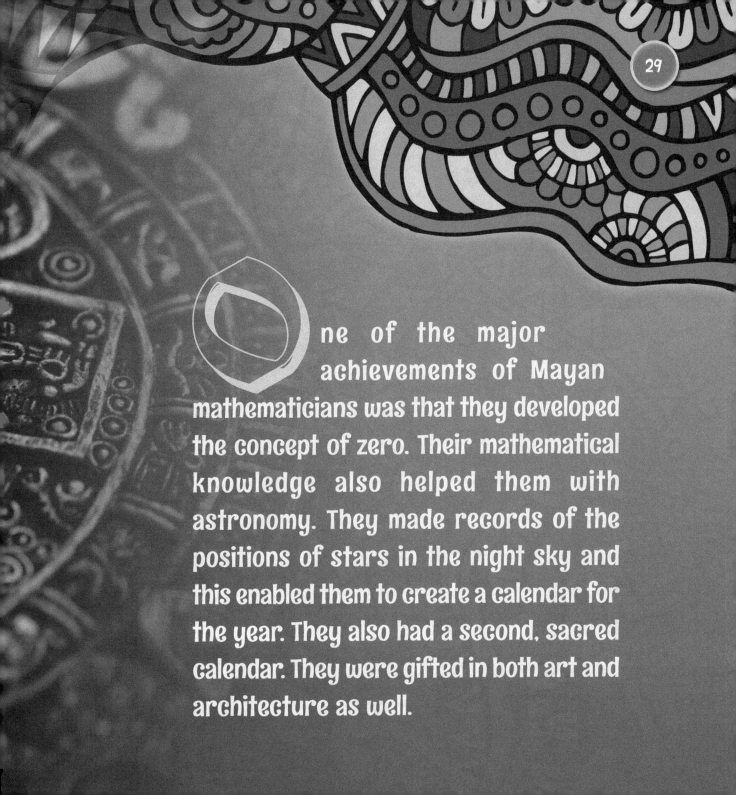

One of the major achievements of Mayan mathematicians was that they developed the concept of zero. Their mathematical knowledge also helped them with astronomy. They made records of the positions of stars in the night sky and this enabled them to create a calendar for the year. They also had a second, sacred calendar. They were gifted in both art and architecture as well.

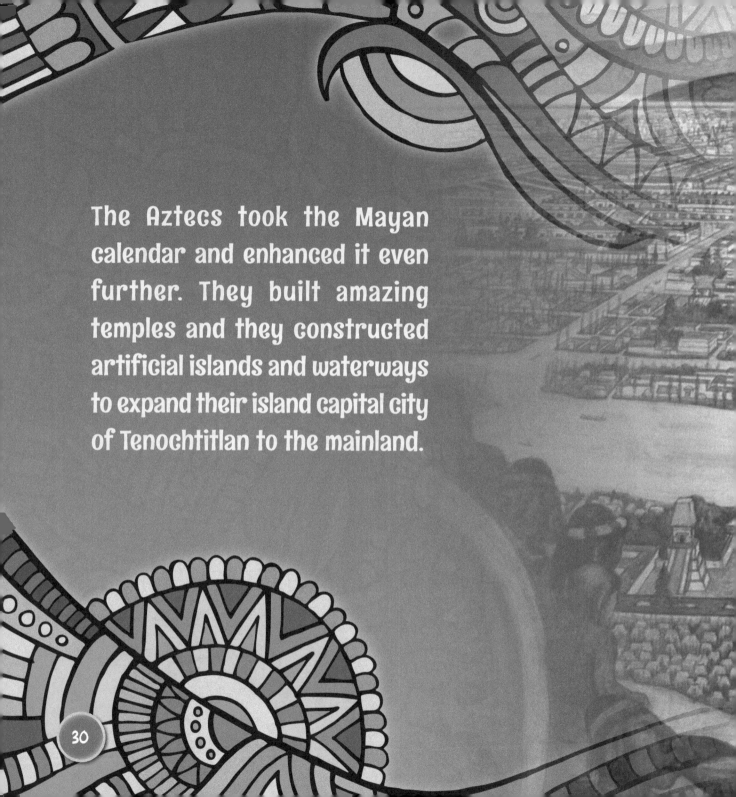

The Aztecs took the Mayan calendar and enhanced it even further. They built amazing temples and they constructed artificial islands and waterways to expand their island capital city of Tenochtitlan to the mainland.

The Aztecs constructed artificial islands and waterways to expand Tenochtitlan to the mainland

Inca agricultural terraces in the
Sacred Valley, Moray in Cuzco, Peru

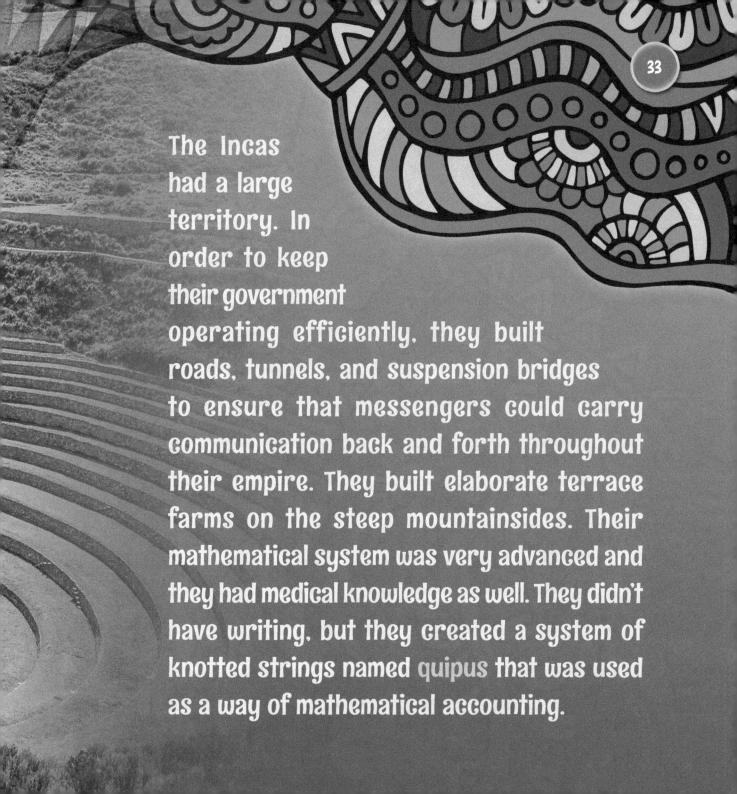

The Incas had a large territory. In order to keep their government operating efficiently, they built roads, tunnels, and suspension bridges to ensure that messengers could carry communication back and forth throughout their empire. They built elaborate terrace farms on the steep mountainsides. Their mathematical system was very advanced and they had medical knowledge as well. They didn't have writing, but they created a system of knotted strings named quipus that was used as a way of mathematical accounting.

Similarities and Differences in Cultural Achievements

Knotted strings named quipus was used as a way of mathematical accounting

All three civilizations were highly advanced. They all had great achievements in the sciences, mathematics, and architecture. They had elaborate forms of art as well. The Mayans and the Aztecs had very similar types of calendars. All three civilizations built beautiful temples. They all had innovations in farming as well. The main difference is that the Mayas and the Aztecs had a solar calendar and systems for writing. The Incas didn't have either of these, but they did have quipus.

How Did Trade Influence These Three Civilizations?

The Mayans had a network of merchants who traveled on rivers, roads and by sea

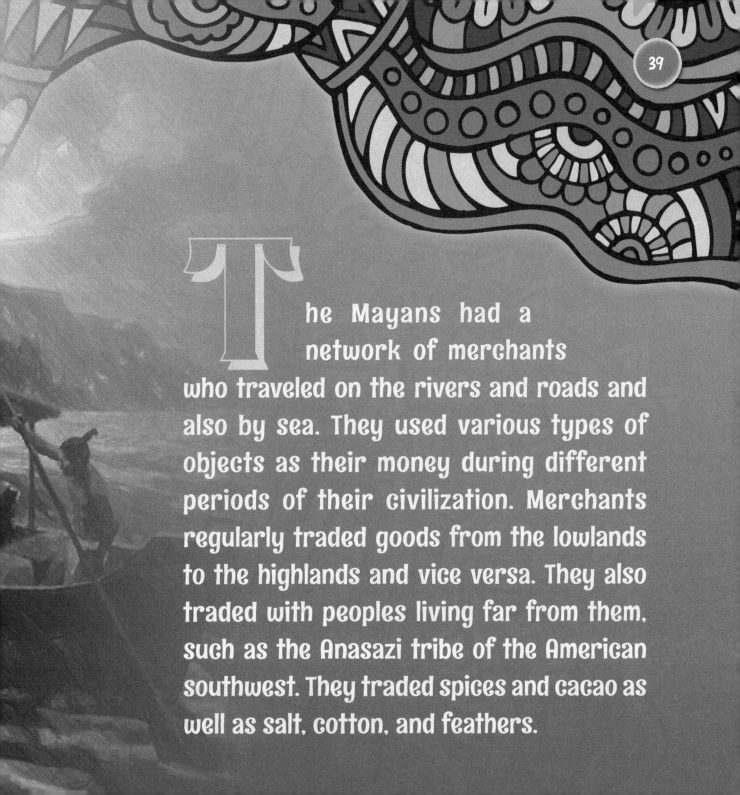

The Mayans had a network of merchants who traveled on the rivers and roads and also by sea. They used various types of objects as their money during different periods of their civilization. Merchants regularly traded goods from the lowlands to the highlands and vice versa. They also traded with peoples living far from them, such as the Anasazi tribe of the American southwest. They traded spices and cacao as well as salt, cotton, and feathers.

The capital city of the Aztecs, Tenochtitlan had enormous markets. On certain market days sometimes more than 50,000 people were there. Trade was central to their economy both for things they needed and luxury items. As their empire conquered surrounding civilizations, they began to trade with this extended group, which also offered them gifts. These actions made their economy expand. They generally traveled by land to make their trades and they traded for rubber, vanilla, and chocolate.

Tenochtitlan marketplace

Today, llamas are still
used to transport goods

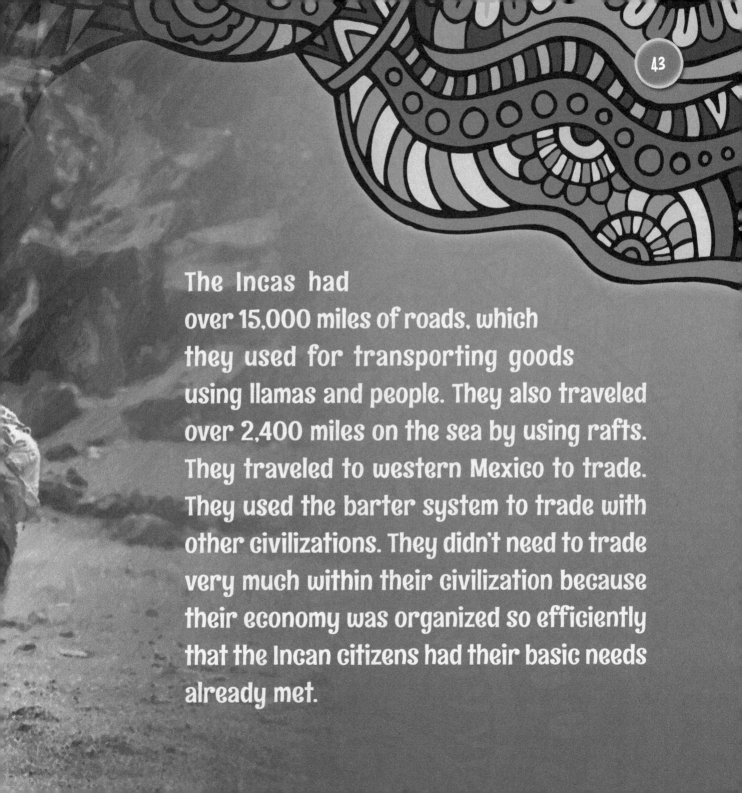

The Incas had over 15,000 miles of roads, which they used for transporting goods using llamas and people. They also traveled over 2,400 miles on the sea by using rafts. They traveled to western Mexico to trade. They used the barter system to trade with other civilizations. They didn't need to trade very much within their civilization because their economy was organized so efficiently that the Incan citizens had their basic needs already met.

Similarities and Differences in How They Traded

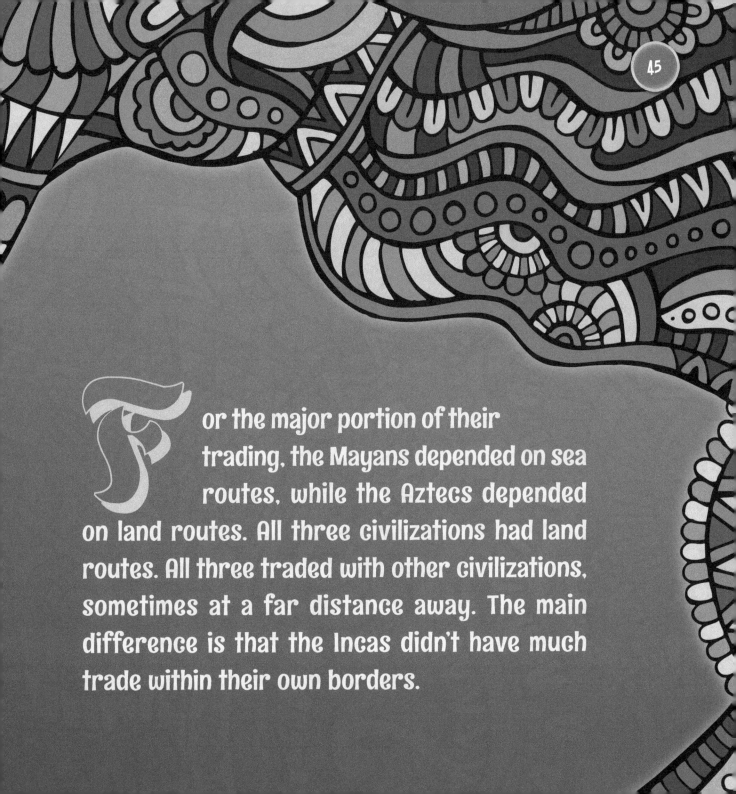

For the major portion of their trading, the Mayans depended on sea routes, while the Aztecs depended on land routes. All three civilizations had land routes. All three traded with other civilizations, sometimes at a far distance away. The main difference is that the Incas didn't have much trade within their own borders.

How Was the Government Set Up in Each Civilization?

The Mayan government was organized by city-states, each of which had its own ruler. The king of each of these city-states helped keep the

Bas Relief depicting K'inich Yax K'uk' Mo' and other ancient Mayan kings

economy running smoothly and he also had importance as a religious figure. The Mayan civilization didn't have one emperor, but instead had several kings.

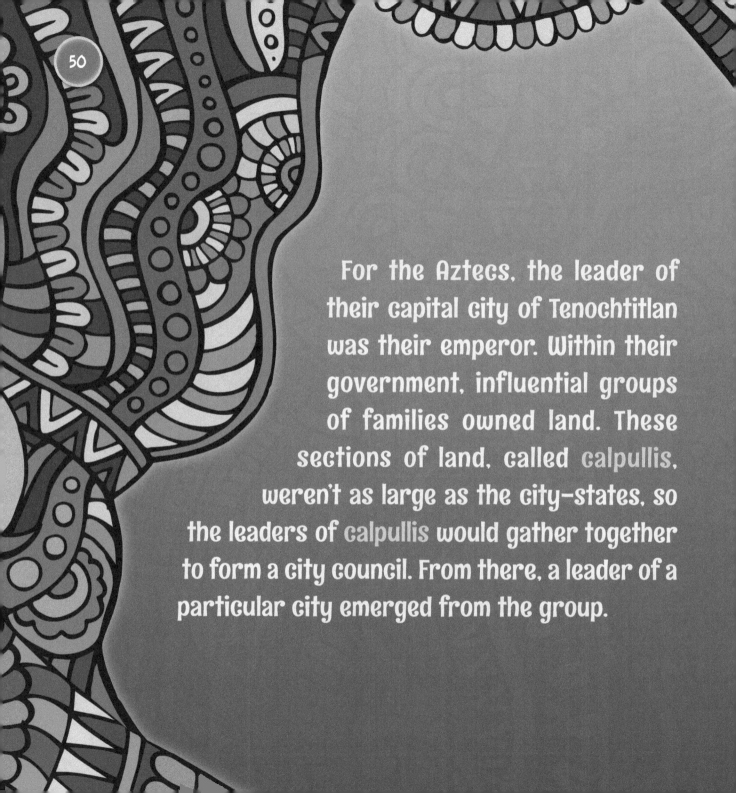

For the Aztecs, the leader of their capital city of Tenochtitlan was their emperor. Within their government, influential groups of families owned land. These sections of land, called calpullis, weren't as large as the city-states, so the leaders of calpullis would gather together to form a city council. From there, a leader of a particular city emerged from the group.

Representation of the Sapa Inca, Pachacuti, wearing the royal crown in the main square of Aguas Calientes, Peru

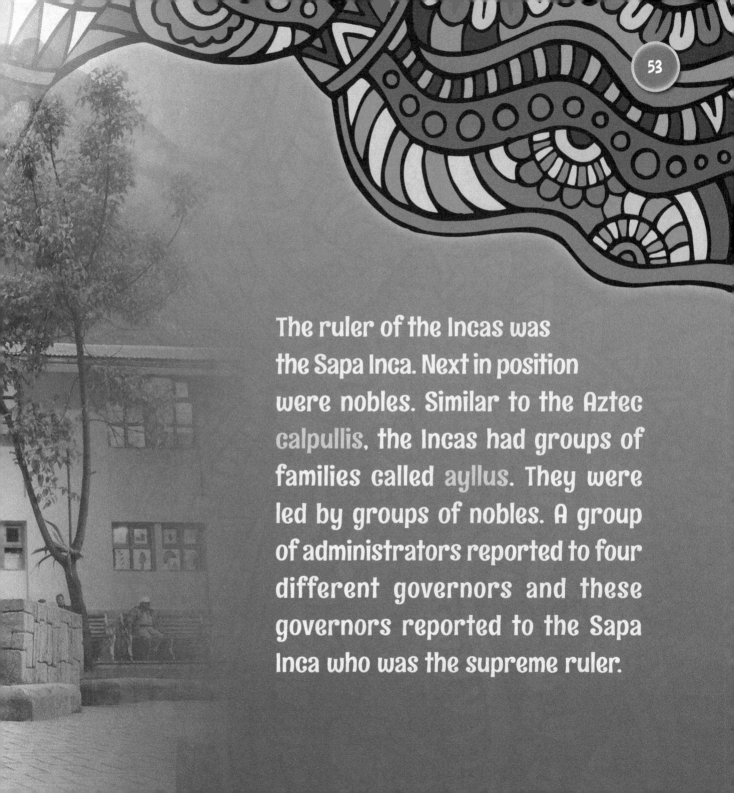

The ruler of the Incas was the Sapa Inca. Next in position were nobles. Similar to the Aztec calpullis, the Incas had groups of families called ayllus. They were led by groups of nobles. A group of administrators reported to four different governors and these governors reported to the Sapa Inca who was the supreme ruler.

Similarities and Differences in Government

All three civilizations had kings. The Aztecs and Incas both had one supreme ruler called an emperor. The Mayans had one king ruler for each city-state. Both the Aztecs and Incas had groups of families as the substructure for their government. The Incas had a very organized government, but the Aztecs allowed people they had conquered to maintain their lifestyle. However, the conquered people were obligated to pay tribute to their captors.

What Were the Religious Beliefs of Each Civilization?

The Mayans built amazing pyramids as their temples. They were polytheistic and believed in more than 150 different deities. Some of the gods were more important than others. They offered riches and blood sacrifices to keep their gods happy.

El Castillo (The Kukulkan Temple) of Chichen Itza, Mayan pyramid in Yucatan, Mexico

Mayan priests were the only ones who had the power to explain the signs and symbols from the gods

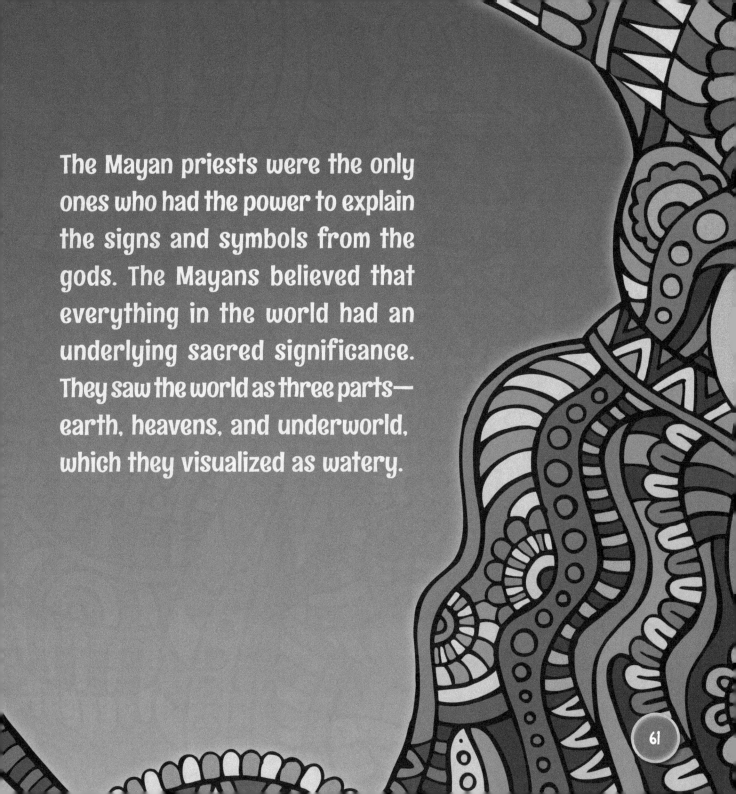

The Mayan priests were the only ones who had the power to explain the signs and symbols from the gods. The Mayans believed that everything in the world had an underlying sacred significance. They saw the world as three parts— earth, heavens, and underworld, which they visualized as watery.

In the Aztec religion, teotl were sacred forces that took the form of goddesses or gods. Three of their most important gods were the god of providence, Tezcatlipoca, the god of wisdom, Quetzalcoatl, and the god of will, Huitzilopochtli.

Huitzilopochtli

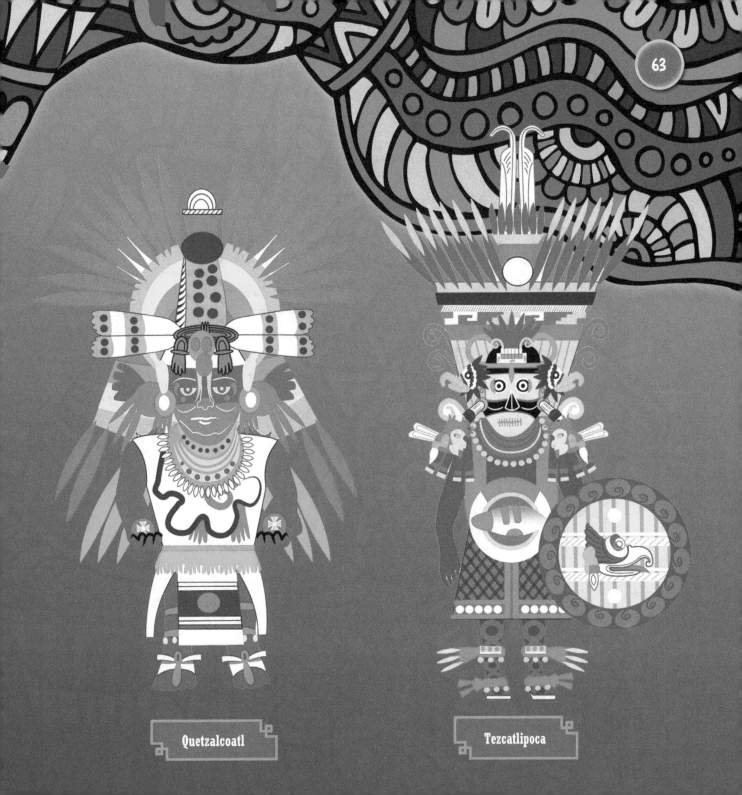

Quetzalcoatl

Tezcatlipoca

Aztec human sacrifice ritual

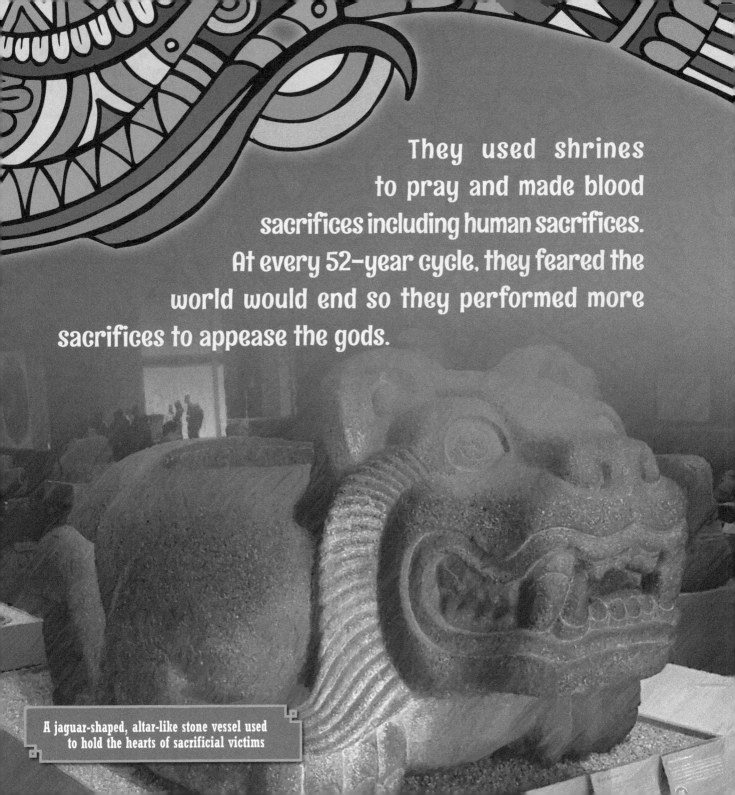

They used shrines to pray and made blood sacrifices including human sacrifices. At every 52-year cycle, they feared the world would end so they performed more sacrifices to appease the gods.

A jaguar-shaped, altar-like stone vessel used to hold the hearts of sacrificial victims

Depiction of a Sapa Inca worshipping Inti in the most important temple in the Inca Empire

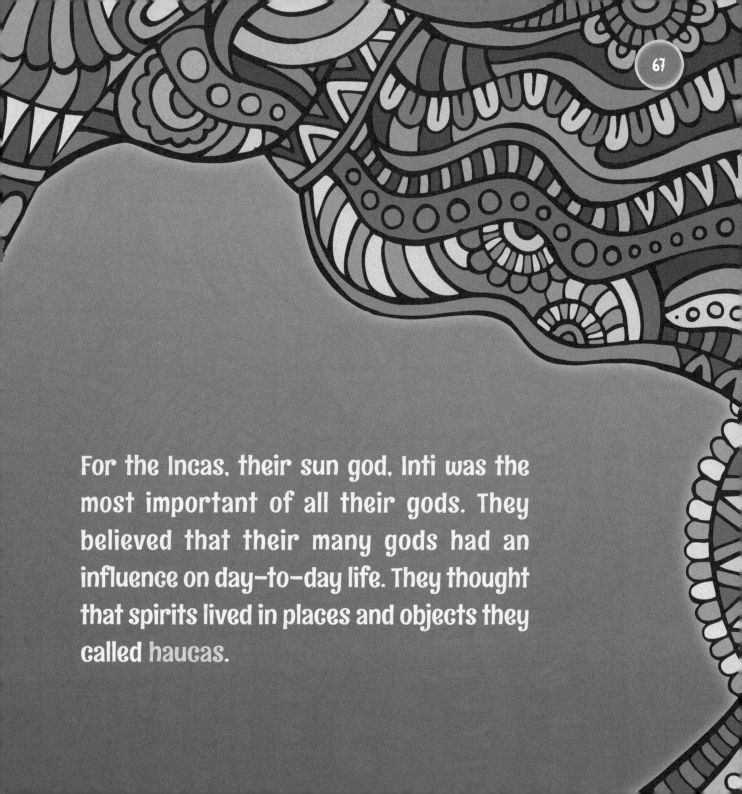

For the Incas, their sun god, Inti was the most important of all their gods. They believed that their many gods had an influence on day-to-day life. They thought that spirits lived in places and objects they called haucas.

They made offerings to the haucas as well as to their gods. They had chosen women as well as priests who predicted future events including the outcome of wars, helped solve crimes, and diagnosed illnesses.

Hauca del Dragon or Dragon Temple

Similarities and Differences of Their Religious Beliefs

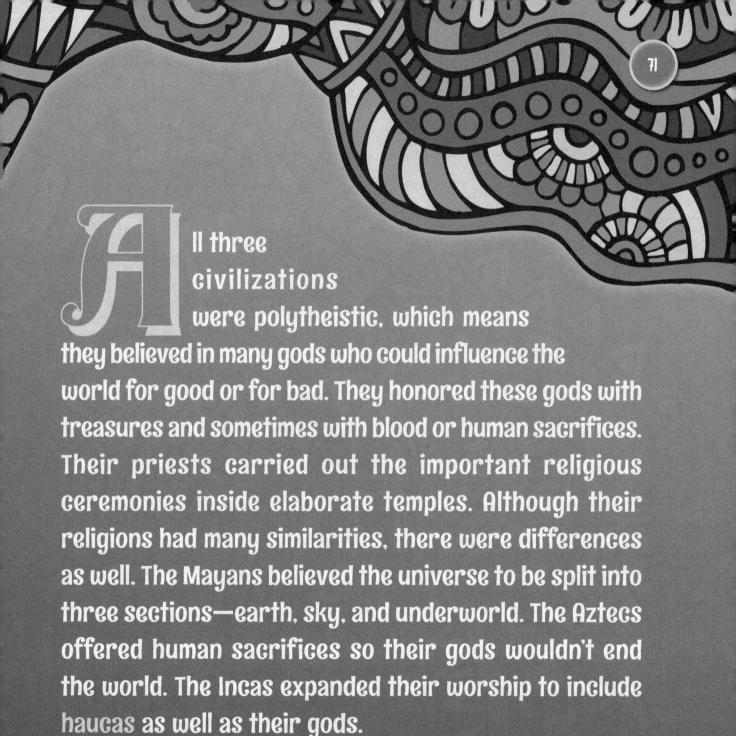

All three civilizations were polytheistic, which means they believed in many gods who could influence the world for good or for bad. They honored these gods with treasures and sometimes with blood or human sacrifices. Their priests carried out the important religious ceremonies inside elaborate temples. Although their religions had many similarities, there were differences as well. The Mayans believed the universe to be split into three sections—earth, sky, and underworld. The Aztecs offered human sacrifices so their gods wouldn't end the world. The Incas expanded their worship to include haucas as well as their gods.

Summary

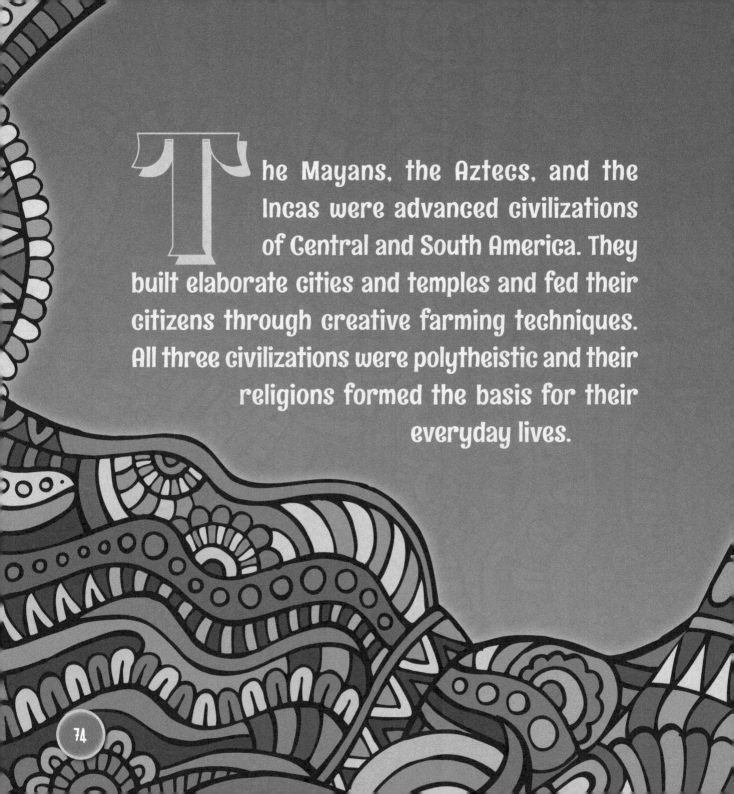

The Mayans, the Aztecs, and the Incas were advanced civilizations of Central and South America. They built elaborate cities and temples and fed their citizens through creative farming techniques. All three civilizations were polytheistic and their religions formed the basis for their everyday lives.

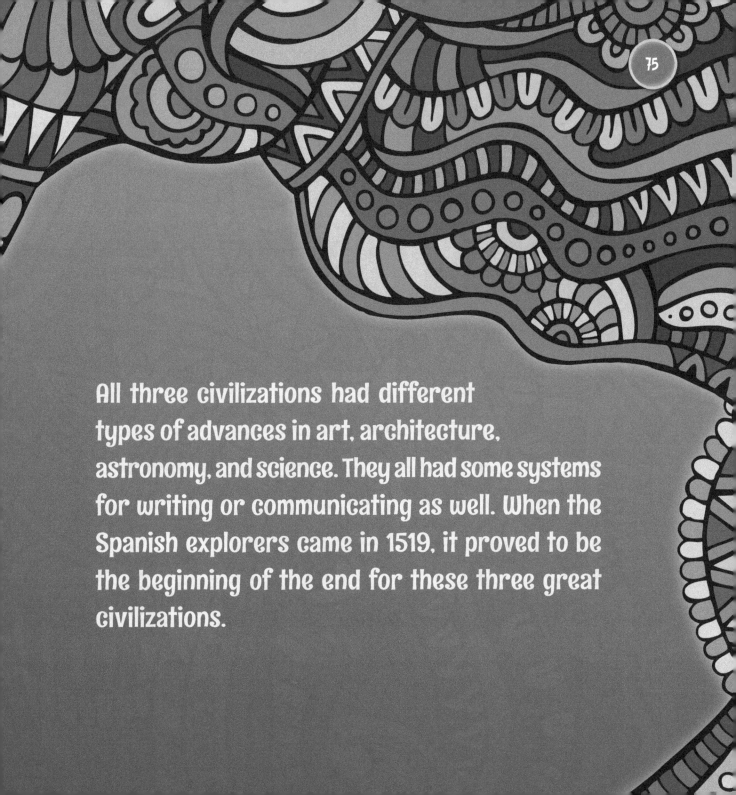

All three civilizations had different types of advances in art, architecture, astronomy, and science. They all had some systems for writing or communicating as well. When the Spanish explorers came in 1519, it proved to be the beginning of the end for these three great civilizations.

Awesome! Now that you've learned about the Aztecs, Incas, and Mayans you may want to read about the history of the Mayan Empire in the Baby Professor book, The History of the Mayan Empire – History Books for Kids | Children's History Books.

Visit

www.SpeedyBookStore.com

To view and download free content
on your favorite subject and browse
our catalog of new and exciting
books for readers of all ages.

CPSIA information can be obtained
at www.ICGtesting.com
Printed in the USA
LVHW011559290520
656908LV00004B/88